MIXED BLESSINGS AND A HEAD FULL OF DREAMS

Mixed Blessings and a Head Full of Dreams

Elane Jackson

ed. Martin Jackson

YOUCAXTON PUBLICATIONS

OXFORD & SHREWSBURY

ISBN 9781911175025
Printed and bound in Great Britain.
Published by YouCaxton Publications

Contents

Bitter Teardrops

So long ago I waited patiently,
Set aside my fears and dismay,
So, so long ago I watched in silence,
As the world passed me by.

So long ago I tried and failed,
I see the others as they progressed each day,
So, so long ago I could hear them say,
How happy they were from day to day.

So long ago with tears I cried,
With bitter teardrops each day passed by,
Then, from a distance, a little light I saw,
Oh! It seemed so long ago.

But with joy comes the sorrow, the bitter, the sweet,
Oh! It seems like yesterday,
I cry as I try to forget the past,
Oh! How I fail, I'm in the past again.

A Beautiful Angel

Today I saw an angel looking straight at me.
She told me that she loves me
And everything will be alright.
I looked into the mirror, and there she was,
This beautiful angel, looking back at me.

I waved my hand and said 'hello'
To this angel looking straight at me.
She waved right back at me and said 'hello', too.
That was when I knew
This beautiful angel was none other than me.

I gave a smile and laughed out loud to think
How lucky I am that God took it upon himself
To give me a perfect gift two hands, two feet,
Two eyes and a beautiful face
And everything in its rightful place.

My Precious Treasure

Oh precious treasured child of mine,
Mine to comfort in distress,
Mine to show by living faith,
Mine to show a Saviour's love,
Mine to punish or reward,
Mine to tell of joys to come,
Mine to chide me when I'm wrong,
Mine to tell me whence I come,
Mine to teach me what I am,
Precious treasure, thou art mine.

A gift from God, a Saviour's love,
Mine to bring right back to Him,
Mine to love and mine to cherish,
This precious gift that God sent me,
I will love and cherish so.
Mine to tell of God's Commandments,
Mine to teach which way to go,
Mine to tell of right and wrong,
Mine to tell of love and hate,
Mine to whisper I love you.

The Race of Life

In this life in which we live, there's a race in which we all must run.
But do you know that those who run in a race,
All run, but only one receives the prize?
But there's a race in which you cannot fail,
                    when striving for eternal life.
Some run for gold, some for silver and some for bronze.
But as for me, I run to receive eternal life.
Just look at your surroundings, and the place in which you live:
Everyone who competes in this game of life
Exercises self-control in all things to win this prize.
So run not with doubt, but with patience,
Not as one that breathes the air, but with certainty,
That the end result is a crown we all shall wear, if we run this race.

It's Not Where You Started

It's not where you started I heard them say,
It is not where you come from,
Or even the place you might have been,
It's not the friends you keep
Or even the place where you might have lived,
It's the place where you ended - that's the trick.

There's always a beginning,
Also an end, a two-way journey,
Where will it end, or where it will it take you?
You alone can tell.
It's not a straight road, nor a mapped-out route.
It's not where you started it's the place where you ended.

You may travel the world, go to different places
That people only dream of, and see different things
That others cannot see.
Yet it's not where you started
But where you will be at the end of the day.
Now you've started the journey, it's up to you where it ends.

The Day is Fast Reviving

Life in all her growing powers,
Spring has now unwrapped the flowers.
Gone is the winter's touch of cold, the frost, and the morning dew.
Seedlings working through the mould,
Making up for the time that was lost.

The days are fast reviving, bestirring, green and strong
The herbs and plants that winter kills no more.
Slumbered at their leisure, the tender flowers,
The stalks, the ear, the full corn at length,
For the sun's now filled the sky, making sure its presence felt.

Running waters ever near, nurturing sun that's lit the sky,
The open flowers, the ripe fruits in the garden green,
The chirping birds that are forever singing,
Fruits to life are forever growing, rich in love, and variety,
The bending branches truly bearing, may they grow till harvest
ceases.

I Remember

I remember when I was just a child sitting
On the back steps, my sister and I,
Watching the trees as they wave in the wind,
Seeing who first could reach the tree
When the mango falls.

Those were the days when we laughed the most,
Rolling around in the grass and having fun,
Watching the gate to see daddy come home
From the field with his leftover food,
Oh, those were the days.

Mother would put the pot on the fire,
Water boiling over, but nothing inside,
God will provide she used to say,
Dinner will be on the table when your father gets home.
Yes, those were the days.

Tucked up in bed, mother kissed us goodnight
Daddy yelling in the back room,
Have you said your prayers?
Silent as lambs beneath the sheet we would hide,
Till mammy and daddy were well out of sight.

When I Can Read

When I can read my name out loud I'll bid farewell
To all my fear, when I smile my tears I'll wipe
And face a frowning world.

When friend betrayed and heart destroyed and fiery
Darts are hurled no more, then I can smile and sing
Out loud, for Satan now has lost his ploy.

When hope restored and love remain, and disappointment
Fears and grief are gone, then, I can smile at Satan's face
For my name is clear, I can read out loud.

I rest me here without a fear, my name I now can read
My heart renewed, my faith restored with confidence
I now can stand, now I have found the hope I've lost.

Where I Live and Where I Work

I look at the surroundings of the place where I live,
I see every day people and every day places.
The neighbours are quiet and the streets are all clean,
And those that we meet are friendly and kind.

Then I venture far off to the place that I work,
Where they are loud and indifferent, and not very nice.
They ask if I'm happy, in the things that I do,
I tell them I'm trying, but I won't tell a lie.

My surroundings are fine, it's just the people I see;
They speak different languages, I can't understand,
So I find a quiet corner, there I sit by myself.
For there I am happy, and write poetry instead.

This Morning

I wake up this morning to the sound of the birds
Tweet, tweet they cry as they chat amongst themselves.

I start the day with a stretch and a yawn,
Before my feet even touch the ground and
Wonder if it's worth it to even get out of bed.

But along came the bird again singing a happy little tune
And that's when I knew I am alive for the birds just told me so.

So I begin my journey to that place I call work
Where the mice are ahead of me in that cold, damp and dusty place.

So I waited till three thirty that's when my shift ends,
Now I'm on my way home again where I can hear the birds sing.
Now I'm all tucked up in bed again feeling comfy and warm.

Out of My Depth

My mouth shall speak of you each day,
My heart beats when I hear your name,
My feet shall walk within your path,
My head fills with mixed emotions when they speak your name.

My eyes open wide when I see your face,
Like a burst of sunshine you make my day bright.
I watch the way you look at me,
With the closeness we share and the love you give.

You reach out your hands but I was out of my depth,
Still I know you will stay ever close by my side.
Out of my depth I'm so in love with you,
Trying to find a place in your heart.

There's a big world out there, but only you fills my mind,
From dawn to dusk all I can see is your face.
I watch the others as they talk about you,
With so much love and adoration.

I see your smile, the look on your face,
As if nothing fazes you, you don't have a care.
Yet, out of my depth I'll always shine,
With you by my side I'll have no fear.

Worship

We come to Him with gladness
And singleness of heart,
We praise His name, we lift Him up
And sing aloud His name.

He loves us when we come to Him
When we seek His grace
For He tells us when we need Him,
Just ask for Him in prayer.

You may not think He answers,
But patience is required.
You may not get what you asked for,
But your prayer He surely answers.

He'll give you what He thinks you need,
Not what He thinks you want.
He'll surely bless you with His love
Your needs He will supply.

In God I Trust

I've long provoked him to his face,
I would not listen to his calls.
But let me now my sins confess,
To him I now commit my ways.
In this dutiful path now I will go.
For now I know he's wise and strong,
And his mighty hands I'm now resting on.
I'll try to please him every day
To help the world around me stand,
To serve and share with patient care
Thy people in their needs I try my best,
To please you, when I am at home or at work.
So fill me with your love and pity.
Now I'm nearing my destination,
For it was your love that found me out
Now I seek no one but you.

A Special Love

There is a special love you have,
More beautiful and sweet,
A tender love like summer springs
That's rich with every flavour it brings.

When morning lights in winter lie
Beneath the clouds that rise
I see a happy family,
More beautiful to know.

Thought of the Day

Don't complain about what you do not have,
Celebrate the things you have.
Give a thought for those who've slept beneath your light,
And those that rummage through your bins.

Just be glad of what you have,
And remember those who do not have.
Remember the man, who took his last fruit up a tree,
And say a prayer before his jump.

He gently peeled his fruit, timely he sit and ate,
And as he slowly dropped the skin
Below him came another man,
Who bent down and picked the skin from off the ground.

Slowly he brushed the dust from off the skin,
Start to eat it with a grin,
Then come the man from off the tree,
Who said, "Thank God there are worse off than me!"

So next time when you think that life is bad,
And the world as done you a wrongful deed,
And you think of giving up,
There's always someone worse off than you. Think again.

No Time to Stand and Stare

We have no time to stand and stare,
No time to give a helping hand to those we meet.
We move around in this world of ours,
With our heads up high in the clouds,
Not knowing what's in front of us,
No word of thanks, nor guilt, nor shame.
Yet life goes on, no matter what,
We have no time to see the wood from the trees.
No time to view the stars in the sky, to see the beauty of the land,
To listen to the birds in the trees as they sing so sweetly,
No time to give a smile to those we meet,
To cheer them on their way, no time to even say hello,
No time to give a little cheer,
We have no time to stand and stare.

No Time to Lose

No time to wait, in this life we live,
No time to give a hand to those we meet.
Yet life has a way of slowing us down,
And showing us what is in store.
If our life were but more simple,
We would have time for those we meet.
But there's no time to wallow in self-pity,
Just time to look ahead.
Time to put what was wrong to right,
To clear the path that was once dark.
To find a place where peace abides,
Yet sweeter still to wake and find
Our lives like sunshine
In the wakening of a brand new day.

Promises

I trust in your judgment and your love
Oh Lord you promise you will love me
No matter what may come, I am glad
You're not like us humans whose venom is like snakes.

They tell you one thing only they mean something else,
So Lord I trust you will forgive me,
Not judge me too harshly,
Lord I am only human and we all make mistakes.

I'm standing on your promises Lord for in them I cannot fail,
I'm leaning on your arms Lord for in them comfort will I find,
I'm depending on your love Lord,
For in it there's joy, and peace of mind.

What Can I Gain

In this world of hate and condemnation
What is there in it to gain?
Yet Jesus left his Father's throne,
Freely he then came to save us from our sins.

Who amongst us would be willing
To do the things that Jesus did?
He disrobed himself to rags, suffered the indignity,
And died for such as you and me.

Amazing love this Christ doth have, that is why I love him so,
He took my sins and my sorrow and now my heart is free.
God has now found me, no riches of earth could have saved me,
His death on the cross was my only salvation.

The guilt on my conscience so heavy has grown
But his blood washed over me and now I am safe in his arms.
The wealth I have is not mine but his,
The whole of creation, of man and beast, belongs to him.

Wings

If wings have I, I would fly so far, far above the sky
I would fly away where there's no trouble in sight
I would go so, so far away and leave no trace in sight.

If wings have I, there's so many places I would go,
Far beyond human reach, I would scale the sky and wander
In the far, far blue yonder, oh if only I had wings.

If wings have I, no rest will I have,
Till I have visited all the places I want to go,
I would fly, fly high, I would fly low.

Till I'm tired of places that I have seen,
Then I would flap my wings and take a rest
But oh, if only I have wings.

Whisper

I whisper a word in the dark of the night,
Not knowing who's listening or if anyone hears me.
I talk to myself, scared out of my wits,
In the dark of the night left alone by myself.

The thunder's now rolling, the lightning is flashing,
And the trees wave to and fro as the wind passes by.
I whisper a word, too scared to go outside,
For the thunder's now bellowing and the storm's fighting back.

There's a knock on the window - who could it be?
The rain's pouring heavily and the clouds are getting dark.
The knocking on the window is getting louder and louder,
And the lighting's still flashing, while the thunder's rolling loud.

The noises are getting closer, as I look through the window
But all I could see was the branches banging on the window pain,
So I hurry back to bed, too scared to venture outside,
And wait until the rain has stopped, and it is safe to go outside.

Neighbourhood Watch

Across the road there sits a man,
Looking to find a shadow he knew so well,
Of a son who went to war.
By night and day he sat and stared,
Looking for his beloved son,
A boy he sent to fight for king and country, a son he dearly loved.

The postman knocks, to his feet he jumps
For news of his son he so dearly missed.
'No news this time', the postman said.
Again he sat waiting patiently, to hear what become of his son,
But in vain he waited, for no one came to put him out of his misery,
To tell him what happened to his only son.

Trying Times

Lord I'm trying my best to stay in your path,
But I am hurting right now,
So please forgive my very thoughts,
I am trying to be good Lord,
But the Devil you see has a way of knowing
How to get the worst out of me.

He's pushing the buttons that makes my heart sad,
So Lord in your mercies,
Keep a tight rein on me.
I'm trying to be humble,
But Satan is always there,
He's egging me on to do the things that I hate.

So I am begging you Lord Jesus,
Please don't turn your back on me,
I trust in your judgment, and the love that you show,
So please dear Jesus keep me in your sight,
For there in your arms, Lord,
I know I am safe.

Picking Up Sticks and Picking Up Stones

Picking up sticks and picking up stones,
All around the town,
Tom fell down and cracked his head
And the stones just rolled away.

Tom, Tom, the whole Town cried,
Your stones have rolled away,
But poor old Tom could not raise his head,
So the stones just rolled and rolled.

So down the hill the whole town went,
To see what they could do.
But the stones just rolled and rolled and rolled,
All the way down the hill.

Remember Me

Remember me when I am gone,
Remember what we talk about.
The places where we have been
The promises that we made together,
The things we said we'd do.

Do not fret for me when I am gone
For my spirit will still be here, watching over you,
Keeping you safe from harm so carry on
And live your life just remember what I say,
And just remember me.

Remember the bad times, remember the good,
Because they both combine together
To strengthen our love. So when I am gone
Just remember this, and think how lucky we were
To have had this time.

Remember me when I am gone,
The joys that we have shared, the fun we had,
The love we shared, the blessing we received.
So don't cry for me, just say good bye,
And live your life for now, until we meet again,
Just promise me that you'll remember me.

Life

When life seems worse than useless
And I wish that I were better off dead,
I take my grief to Jesus,
For his love has never failed.

He promises he will call me,
His words are strong and true.
So I put my trust in his love,
For his love will conquer all.

Sometime the clouds of sorrow overtake me
No matter what I do,
So I kneel and pray, in confessing,
Yet still, He whispers, I love you.

Morning Dew

At the break of dawn when the sun comes up,
The glittering light on the dew shone so bright,
Like sparkling diamonds, gems so refined,
These drops of water, like a chain of pearls.

Then along come the butterflies in their splendid array,
Formation flying in a beautiful display.
From flower to flower they fly to each one,
As they disperse and diffuse in colours to delight.

The dew on the flowers drips little by little,
Like a fountain display when the water falls.
The buds on the roses open wide as to say
Thank you for helping me on this bright sunny day.

Gifts of Words

Words have a longer life than deeds,
Words are powerful. Words can destroy,
Yet words are a gift if you know how to use it,
Speak it with confidence, speak with authority,
Words can be tolerated, words can be wise
A love of words can be used,
But actions speak louder than words themselves.
Words can teach us, words can encourage us.
It's an instruction for life, use it wisely.
Don't let it condemn you,
Words cannot be retracted once you speak them out,
For words are powerful tools.
Words are life.

Love

Love is a choice we choose to act upon,
Whether we feel it or not.
Sometimes we love in fear,
Sometimes we love just because we need to be loved.
But love is a word, yet it comes from the heart.
Love can kill, love can sentence,
Love can condemn, love can rebuild,
Love is patient, love is kind,
Love is everlasting it has no end.
But most of all love comes from within,
Love and hate join together,
I love you. I hate you, where will it end?
But if it's true love, it will always shine through,
Love will lead the way. Love conquers all.

The Moon

In the distant land so far away
I watch the blue sky turn to grey.
I watch the stars as they come out to play,
As if by magic they appear.

I watch the moon as it takes its place,
Shining brightly in the sky.
I see clouds as they gather around
As if to welcome the moon.

The glittering stars they shine so bright,
Just like diamonds in the skies.
I look around and there it is,
This big bright orb, that lights the skies.

A Promised Love

This is the promise of his love
That he would stand by me.
There is a kindness in his voice,
A sweetness in his touch.

He said our lives would be all sunshine,
Our love would be entwined beyond belief.
His voice of love, is the gentlest tone,
When he whispered 'I love you'.

Although I often seem to be alone,
My life my love still stands by me.
He has kept his promise and his love,
The love that I now keep.

I'll take comfort in knowing this:
That I'll be beside him all the time.
His face, his smile, his gentle touch
Has now made my life complete.

A Place in the Sun

Who more than self their country love
Undimmed by human tears?
With bodies which explode in war
A place where there's no peace,
But a place in the sun you always find,
That self nor love cannot destroy.
To men and nations come the moaning
When blood is shed in vain;
And though the cause of evil prospers,
The truth alone will stand.
There is a choice that you can take -
In which direction you will choose.
There is light and there is darkness -
Just remember this - in the light of day,
Jesus is in control.

A Sister's Prayer

We pray for them that did the wrong
Like him with pardon on his tongue,
They climb the steepest ascended hill
And mock his cross, his robe and all.

We pray for those who stand by him,
And for those who watch their master whipped
In shame; a noble man, who did no wrong,
Yet mocked and scorned to the very end.

We pray for those who called on him
To save their sorry lives.
A kingly crown was set on him
To follow in his father's land.

If I were a Magician

If I were a magician, what would I do?
I don't think I'd paint the world pink or blue.
The colour of summer, the colour of spring,
Just goes to show a magician has a hand in everything.

Things from the past I'd zap right away,
But then, where would I be today?
Left alone with no present, no past
And nothing that lasts.

A world of glitter, a world of gold,
But what would happen when I grow old?
A magician's work is hard to do,
They make things appear in front of you.

Hearts and spades is a game of charades,
Rabbit in a box and out it pops.
Flowers and gifts a shifty sight,
Now you see it and now you don't.

A wand that magics things and tricks,
A welcome sight for the eye to see.
A handkerchief that has no end,
Jack-in-a-box, that's your lot.

I'd change the world, the poor and the lame,
I'll let them see what a good magician I am.
No need to worry I would say,
I'd snap my finger and the work would be done.

With a wand in my hand I would strike a blow,
To a troublesome world I'll take my stand.
I'll have my wand to help those who are in need,
For a good magician that's who I am.

A Suffering Child

When I remember the days of old
How I suffered and was consumed with grief.
How weary I was with my mourning
And my night and day were filled with tears.

A suffering child I now become.
My mother has been taken away from me,
My eyes are now so full of tears,
My voice has become hoarse because of my weeping.

I heard them singing the night she died a song, I'll never forget:
'Earth hath no sorrow that God cannot cure'.
Yet there was no cure for my dear loving mother,
Who died, and left us all behind.

An Outcry

It's a strange place to stay since our mother died,
With a father, no love, a family who don't care,
With siblings who cannot share my pain,
No-one to run to nowhere to hide,
It's such a strange place since our mother died.
From pillar to post I was pushed, and shoved.
It seems I have been to the four corners and back
Yet no-one wants me, no-one seems to care,
Eight sisters, three brothers to be exact.

Still no-one to comfort me, to say
'Come little sister there's a place in my home'.
It's such a sad place since our mother has died.
Then from a far distance a sister, I was told,
One who will love me and see I'm alright,
So I travelled to London, to this far away place,
Where I'm settled and happy with kids of my own.
Now I can look back to the place where I'm from,
And think of my poor mother with memories of love.

Across the Bridge

Across the bridge, I saw you standing,
The sun shining down on your face,
And the wind blowing through your hair.
I watch you as you gaze into space,
Wondering what's on your mind.

I watch you as you smile at the passers-by,
Hoping you would catch a glance of me.
I study your face - the way you smile
And the glitter that comes from your eye.
If only you would turn and look at me.

Across the bridge there's only four steps away.
Just reach out your hands and I'll be there.
My heart beating faster and my legs trembling too,
Across the bridge -
That's where you'll find me.

Behind the Mask

Behind the mask there stood a man
Full of fear, full of hate.
He stood alone, sword in hand,
To fight for what he thought was right.
Yet behind the mask no-one could tell
How scared he was, or who he is.
Yet though he was frightened
He was brave enough to take upon himself
A fight he knew he could not win.
Behind this mask was just a boy, full of life,
Yet full with hate, he hid his face.
So no one could tell how angry and resentful
He was with them.
Yet alone he stood,
To brave the world
To let them know his presence felt.

Be Strong

When all around you seems to fail,
And nothing seems to go your way,
Don't give up, just push ahead,
And victory will be yours.

The going may get tough,
And every way seems dark
Just be strong and push ahead –
Victory is in sight.

But bear in mind that no discovery
Is made from a shallow ground.
You have to dig and dig and dig
And you will surely win.

Just pray united, something will happen.
Be strong, be brave, just push ahead.
A little bit harder and you will win.
Around the corner there's victory to be won.

Homeward Bound

Like a bird in the sky far away from its nest,
I have wandered away from home.
I travel around, looking for what they call peace
But all I find is discomfort and pain.
Then I think of my poor mum
And how she must have felt,
And then I think of homeward bound.
Then my dear old mum calls me home where I belong.
Now I am safe in her arms, and her love
That brought me home.

I Hear I Feel I Know

I hear they say that time will tell
Of how you live and how you walk.
I hear they say that life's a drag but
How I feel I just don't know.

I feel that life will pass me by,
I have no way of finding out,
I see so many traps and pits
But how I feel I just don't know.

I know that life is what you make it,
Yet I'm sure that is a farce, I heard some
Say life is full of fun, but surprisingly
I hear, I feel, but I just don't know.

If Only

If only I do, this is a favourite password for mankind.
I would do this and I wouldn't have done that,
If only I had stopped to think,
I would have done this,
If only I had stayed here
I wouldn't have to go there.

If only if only I could hear them say,
I would try to be this, not try to be that,
With tears running down and the record
Still scratching, all you could hear is
I wish I did this,
Then I wouldn't have to do that.

If only I know this I wouldn't,
I wouldn't do that.
If only I start here,
I wouldn't end up over there,
Oh if only I knew
Then ....

Seek the Good in Others

Do not judge, or speak evil of others, but look for the good in them.
Do not imitate evil, but imitate that which is good.
Don't act on impulse, but act on the truth.
For squabbling over trivial matters gives way to Satan's power.

Seek the good in others don't look for the worst in them.
So when you are faced with a difference of opinion try and work
it out.
Try and see the best in others, and remember,
Our goal is to build each other up not to tear each other down.

Speak to Me

Speak to me that I may speak
Let me love thee more and more.
Lead me gently, gently as I go,
Until my very heart overflows.
Put not a seal upon my lips,
Just let me slowly do thy will.

Speak to me while life shall last,
Let me know thy perfect love.
Speak to me, oh speak to me
Until my soul is lost in your love.
Speak to me just as thou will,
And when, and where.

Speak to me that I may hear,
That I may be calm to comfort thee.
Let me be still and murmur not,
Strong and brave to face thy foe.
Speak to me, that all may see
That true love conquers all.

Stay Awhile

Stay awhile and reap God's blessing
Of the gifts he promised us.
Just be ready to receive him
He is waiting patiently.

Stay awhile don't be in a hurry,
For you'll miss his precious love.
He is willing to redeem you
If you only let him in.

Patiently he now awaits you,
He will set you free from sin.
He has died to bring salvation,
To the rich and to the poor.

He don't care about your background,
Neither where you have been,
He has such a forgiving nature,
He will wash away your sin.

He is tugging at your heart string,
Won't you let the saviour in?
He is willing he is able
If you only let him in.

You don't need to tarry any longer.
He is waiting at the door.
He is knocking, knocking, knocking,
Just open your heart and let him in.

Yesterday

Yesterday is past and gone
Tomorrow may not come.
So on your journey,
Just greet someone,
Let them know you care,

Let them know they're not alone,
Just a little smile will do.
Today is now a brand new day.
Give a thought for those you see,
Wave a hand, just say hello.

Put a smile on someone's face,
And don't forget that life is short.
It can be taken in a flash.
So in your rush, just give a thought
For those you passed by in a rush.

Tell it Like it is

I'll speak my mind, I'll tell the truth.
Some folk hate me just for that,
They say I am too outspoken, too brash.
But I just speak the truth,
And I tell it like it is.

I have worked hard in everything I do,
I do my best not to let anyone down,
Some say I am too up front, too familiar
But I say I speak my mind,
And I tell it like it is.

I'll take a stand when I am in the right
I let them know just how I feel.
I'll keep my cool when I am in the wrong,
I will say sorry if it's my fault, but I will not be silent.
I will tell it like it is.

No Time to Dwell in the Past

No time to dwell in the past I would say,
No time to think of the things that led me astray.
The things that make me apart from the rest,
The things that put me in a rut.

The past is gone, the present is now
The future looks bright through the tunnel ahead,
Yet the past lingers on, there's nowhere to hide,
I try to look forward, but the past catches up.

Then I think of the life that I now have,
The happiness and the joy I now feel,
With the past to tell me where I'm coming from
And the future to tell me where I'm at.

I can't forget the past,
But I can surely learn from it.
For the past is gone,
And the future is now.

Just a Word

Love is a word often used by all.
No-one seems to know how it works.
I love you, I love you, what does it mean,
How do you use it, or how does it show?

A warm liking or affection some say will do,
While some think of sex a passion they call love.
Love is romantic some say is true,
While some say love is forgiving maybe a kiss or two.

Love, love, how easy it comes - I love you today.
Tomorrow is another day, where is the love then I say?
An affair or two, a love child in the process.
How do I know what is love, and when will I know?

The Church

The church has one foundation
Built by God for one and all,
Built to do the Lord's bidding,
To praise His name and honour Him.

The foundation is the body of Christ
The people whom He chose,
Those that accept Him,
The people they call saints.

Those who will forsake all
And follow after Him,
The church is the foundation
Which is Jesus Christ the lord.

He is the creator
Of all things that are made.
Whether they be great or small,
He made them in His image.

In His image did He create them all,
His love He injected in us,
And then He did the bravest thing,
He gave His life for all.

If Only I Was Young Again

If only I was young again,
I would have listened to what my mother said.
I would have stayed in school you see,
Till I did well, with honours too.
I would never have done the things I've done
Or walk the path that I have trod.
I would have learnt and studied harder,
I would be the best that I now seek.

I would have stayed in school you see,
Not make a fuss, nor trouble seek,
For now I have learnt the hardest way.
There is only one thing now that I would keep
The latest love that I now have,
The one that swept me off my feet,
The one that makes my life complete.
Oh if only I was young again.

Voices

His voice I heard now saddens me,
I must confess I love him still.
But his face I see as if by chance,
A smile so false at his glance I retreat.

I follow my heart and spoil the plot,
I set my foolish battered heart free,
For no more will I let my heart rule my head,
For this voice I hear no more bothers me.

Better late than never, some would say,
I'm free as a bird, free to choose, free to live.
For now you see, I have conquer my fear,
The past no more troubles me.

Restore my Faith

Restore my faith in the human race, let me not be dismayed.
For no-one has ever hated his own child,
Let us now encourage one another to be more like you,
For you have loved us every day,

Let our love and willingness to forgive be our constant aim,
Some may choose to forget oh Lord, but kindness is the key,
Your words assure us of a promise that you have left behind
Restore our mind and our heart then show us the way.

The Lost Sheep

'Baa-baa', said Nelly the sheep, 'have you seen my mum?'
'Moo-moo', said Bertie the cow, 'have you tried the barn?'
'Nay- nay', said Billy the goat, 'she's in the field next door.'

'Baa-baa, thank you sir', said Nelly the sheep,
'Baa-baa', skipping and jumping she ran to find her mother,
'Baa-baa', she ran into Mr. Jolly the fox.

'My dear', said Mr. Jolly the fox, 'are you on your own?'
'Baa-baa', said Nelly the sheep, 'my mum is over there.'
'BAA- BAA', she shouted so loud, Mr. Jolly the fox just ran away.

Prophesy

I see my life in front of me
Not knowing what the future holds.
I would pay to hear my fortune told,
To know how I'd be when I grow old.

But each fortune teller tells a different tale:
Some of fortune of a different kind, some tell of love,
Of riches untold, some tell of the past,
But that's water under the bridge.

But hope springs eternal, even though it might be in short supply,
So I'll make a wish or two, otherwise it would be too easy
To sacrifice my dream for the sake of someone else's gold.
So instead I'll wait for life's givings to see what is in store for me.

Eager Steps

From every stormy wind that blows,
There's calm, a sure retreat,
From every swelling of the seas,
To every eager step we take,
Our trials will pass,
Our joys will be complete.
This is my soul-inspiring song:
With courage, bold, these words I write,
Then weep I no more, my work is done,
For this I am sure, the prize I have won.

Looking Too Far

Don't look too far into the future
Keep appreciating the blessings in your life,
No looking back to see how things might have been,
Just focus on the here and now,
And the prophecy will fulfil.

Don't waste time and energy trying to be someone you're not,
Don't live for tomorrow, just live one day at a time.
Don't be too hasty looking too far ahead,
For that will cause a problem, you cannot fathom why;
So live for today and tomorrow will take care of itself.

City Life

In this ever changing world,
Full of people full of hope, full of dreams,
Daily born and growing old,
Living, dying, in this ever changing world below.

But in the bustle of this city
Life is set a million fold,
With people searching for fame and glory,
Some for love that passed them by.

Some seek for a fortune they will not find,
While some hold on to the past,
And try to look too far forward,
Others spell out where they stood.

In this urban wilderness
The old are dying,
The young are changing,
In their latest trendy craze.

Lyrics changing, guitar playing,
Hip-hop on the radio,
People dancing, children playing,
In this their ever changing world.

Run, Run, Run

Hiding scared and frightened,
With no place to go but underground,
Listening out for every footstep,
Every movement, every sound.

Escaping father was my only option,
Stay and die, was his cry.
A door slammed shut, every window bolted,
Keeping me out, that was his motto.

The daily paper he would say,
Would tell of my early demise if I didn't go.
So he showed me to the door, and walked away.
He gave me a choice, I chose to live.

No looking back, no regret.

Days Gone By

Today I looked around me
And thought of days gone by,
And wondered where the years have flown
And where I am today.

Life is full of its ups and downs
In every walk of life,
Yet I caught a glimpse of yesterday,
A moment frozen in time.

I heard the sparrows in the trees,
I watched the snowflakes,
They fall to the ground,
Then in a moment they were gone.

I saw the sunshine in the sky,
The rainbow spread across the land,
I watched the day turn into night
Another moment had gone by.

Tomorrow is just another day,
For some it may not come.
And so I thought of days gone by
When life was full of fun.

I cannot tell what the future holds,
That's one thing that is sure.
So I live for the here and now,
These golden moments I will treasure.

A Cherished Love

Do not cry, don't shed any tears
Just be thankful for the time you shared.
He may be gone, but he's still here,
In every walk you take.

A mirrored love that you both shared
The simple smiles you shared.
This precious gift that God gave you
Was only for a while.

Just remember the things you shared,
And the happiness he brought.
The little things that made you smile,
The things that made you cry.

And think how lucky you have been
To have known such love
In a cherished son.
Be happy .....

Dedicated to Donald Vincent on the loss of his son

The Way Things Were

Each night before we go to bed
There comes a knock upon our doors,
There stood a man whose rules were strict,
A man I knew to be my Dad.
The windows shut, the bolted doors,
That was my father's nightly chores.

At eight each night he watched us pray,
We never knew just what to say.
He never kissed us on our cheeks,
"Goodnight" was all he said to us.
Then he shut the door and moved away,
And off he went until the very next day.

At dawn each day before the cock would crow,
There comes the knock again.
There stood my father at the door.
 "Devotion time" he shouts out loud,
Day after day, night after night, that knock would come,
Not even a whisper, but a shout.

The Boy Next Door

Through my window I could see
The boy who lives next door.
He hangs his kite upside down
Beneath his window ledge.

His two best friends who visit him,
They make the neighbours mad,
They scream and shout like silly lads
And tease the neighbour's dogs.

There is a tree next to the fence, its branches over spread.
They climb across the neighbour's fence and jump into their yard,
The frightened cat scarpers away
Never to be seen again.

Staying Power

As dew falls upon the tender herbs
Diffusing fragrance all around,
So is the love that for me he gives,
Confirmed and sealed for evermore.

Through each perplexing path of life,
Our love will guide our wandering eyes,
As showers that usher in the spring,
With water that quenches the thirsty ground.

Though his arms around me are strong,
That perfection scares me so,
A look of love, a hand held tight,
That's how it will stay for my true love and I.

www.ingramcontent.com/pod-product-compliance
Lightning Source LLC
Chambersburg PA
CBHW021143020426
42331CB00005B/872